Garfield Weighs in

BY: JIM DAVIS

BALLANTINE BOOKS · NEW YORK

Happy Birthday
Pete
Jan 1989
From
Grams & Pop

Library of Congress Catalog Card Number: 81-69192
ISBN 0-345-32010-7

Manufactured in the United States of America

First Ballantine Books Edition: March 1982

30 29 28 27 26 25

4-9

I THINK I'LL STEP INTO THE NEXT ROOM AND HAVE A NERVOUS BREAKDOWN

JIM DAVIS

WHAT'S WARM AND FUN TO LIE IN...

JIM DAVIS

4-10

AND MUST BE CHASED, BUT CAN'T BE CAUGHT?

LEAVE THAT CHICKEN LEG ALONE, GARFIELD. IT'S MINE

© 1980 United Feature Syndicate, Inc.
SMACK!

WHACK!
SPLAT!
JIM DAVIS

IT'S THINGS LIKE THIS THAT TEND TO DIMINISH MY ENTHUSIASM FOR OWNING A CAT
4-13

EAT UP, PAL

© 1980 United Feature Syndicate, Inc.

5-2

JIM DAVIS

I WON'T SAY GARFIELD IS FAT, BUT THE LAST TIME HE GOT ON A FERRIS WHEEL, THE TWO GUYS ON TOP STARVED TO DEATH

SPLAT!

© 1980 United Feature Syndicate, Inc.

5-3

I MUST SPEAK TO JON ABOUT CHANGING THE WATER IN MY BOWL

JIM DAVIS

WHAT'S HAPPENING?
I HAVE NO URGE TO SHOVE ODIE OFF THE TABLE!

5-4

I'M LOSING MY TOUCH!

I MUST BE HAVING AN ATTACK OF NICE!
© 1980 United Feature Syndicate, Inc.

PUSH

WITH SELF-CONTROL YOU CAN CONQUER ANYTHING
JIM DAVIS

GARFIELD! WHY WOULD YOU EVER WANT TO CATCH THAT FISH?

© 1980 United Feature Syndicate, Inc. 5-16

SOME PEOPLE **LOVE** CATS FOR WHAT THEY **ARE**...

AND SOME PEOPLE **ARE** CATS FOR WHAT THEY **LOVE**

JIM DAVIS

© 1980 United Feature Syndicate, Inc. 5-17

WHAT'S THE MATTER, JON? CAT GOT YOUR TONGUE?

YOU MIGHT THAY THAT

JIM DAVIS

MY PIANO'S POSSESSED!
THERE'S AN EVIL SPIRIT
IN MY PIANO!

YOU TAKE
THAT BACK!

I'LL JUST TAKE THE LAST HELPING OF LASAGNA, GARFIELD

5-23 © 1980 United Feature Syndicate, Inc.

AND YOU MAY DO WHATEVER YOU WISH WITH THE PAN, HA-HA

WHANG!

SPLAT!

JIM DAVIS

I'M GETTING TIRED OF YOUR STRONG-ARM TACTICS AROUND HERE, GARFIELD

5-24

REMEMBER: BLESSED ARE THE MEEK: FOR THEY SHALL INHERIT THE EARTH

BUT, IN THE MEANTIME, THE STRONG WILL MAKE A PRETTY COMFORTABLE LIVING

© 1980 United Feature Syndicate, Inc. JIM DAVIS

GRAB!

STRETCH

PTING!

KABOING!

ZOOM!

FLAP FLAP FLAP

THAT'S THE DARNDEST THING I'VE EVER SEEN

© 1980 United Feature Syndicate, Inc.

JIM DAVIS

5-25

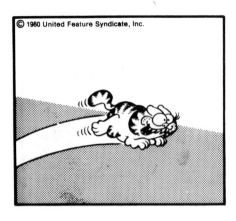
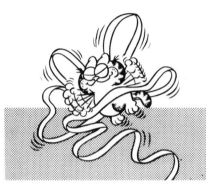

SPLOOT!

WHAT'S THAT?

LEMON MERINGUE ODIE

JIM DAVIS © 1980 United Feature Syndicate, Inc.

♪ HERE, ODIE!

5-29 © 1980 United Feature Syndicate, Inc.

I'M GOING TO TRAIN YOU TO SIT UP TODAY

IT'S HARD TO TEACH A DEAD DOG NEW TRICKS

JIM DAVIS

SOME PEOPLE SAY I'M MEAN TO ODIE. DON'T GET ME WRONG, I **LOVE** DOGS. AND IF I'M LYING, MAY LIGHTNING ...

5-30 © 1980 United Feature Syndicate, Inc.

STRIKE THE DOG NEXT DOOR

KERPOW!
YIP!

JIM DAVIS

TO PROPERLY ENJOY TENNIS YOU MUST HAVE THE CORRECT STANCE

5-31

YOU'LL HAVE TO IMAGINE THE EASY CHAIR, TV, AND SIX-PACK

JIM DAVIS © 1980 United Feature Syndicate, Inc.

SLURP!

YUK

LOOK, ODIE... ME CAT, YOU DOG, WE FIGHT. THAT'S THE ORDER OF THINGS

6-8

UNDERSTAND?

SLURP!

© 1980 United Feature Syndicate, Inc.

JIM DAVIS

THE JUNGLE CAT AWAKES WITH A VORACIOUS APPETITE

© 1980 United Feature Syndicate, Inc.

6-9

HE INSTINCTIVELY SETS OUT TO SLAY SOME BREAKFAST

GARFIELD

THAT WASN'T VERY PRETTY, BUT IT'S ALL PART OF THE FOOD CHAIN

JIM DAVIS

GARFIELD

THE ALLEY CAT SCROUNGES FOR FOOD

6-10

HE POKES HIS HEAD INTO A PROMISING GARBAGE CAN

PEEEYEWWW!

© 1980 United Feature Syndicate, Inc.

JIM DAVIS

THE WILD CAT STALKS THE ENVIRONS IN SEARCH OF PREY

6-11

HE ATTACKS A HELPLESS CHICKEN

A BIG, **BIG**, ONLY SEMI-HELPLESS CHICKEN

JIM DAVIS   © 1980 United Feature Syndicate, Inc.

THE FARM CAT SETS OUT TO PATROL HIS PROPERTY

© 1980 United Feature Syndicate, Inc.   6-12

HE HAPPENS UPON A PLOT OF FRESH CATNIP

AND WAKES UP THE NEXT MORNING IN ATLANTIC CITY WITH A BARBIE DOLL

JIM DAVIS

THE ACTOR CAT IS BEING FILMED ESCAPING FROM THE ENEMY

6-13

© 1980 United Feature Syndicate, Inc.

HE MUST LEAP OFF A CLIFF TO COMPLETE THE ESCAPE

WHICH, OF COURSE, IS DONE BY A STUNT DOG

JIM DAVIS

THE HOUSE CAT HAS A BUSY SCHEDULE

© 1980 United Feature Syndicate, Inc.

6-14

WHAT WITH SHARPENING CLAWS

AND SEEING HIS OWNER OFF ON A BIG NIGHT

JIM DAVIS

6-22

JIM DAVIS

© 1980 United Feature Syndicate, Inc.

WHEW. I CAN'T FINISH MY MEAL

6-23

WHAT AM I SAYING ?!!

IT JUST WOULDN'T BE GARFIELD TO LEAVE FOOD

© 1980 United Feature Syndicate, Inc. JIM DAVIS

JIM DAVIS   © 1980 United Feature Syndicate, Inc.

WHUMP!

6-24

DARN.
I CAN'T
SLEEP

SLUP

MILK

PUFF
PUFF

© 1980 United Feature Syndicate, Inc.   6-29

JIM DAVIS

OH NO! HERE COMES THE SLUDGE MONSTER!

7-4 © 1980 United Feature Syndicate, Inc.

ARRGH!

I WISH YOU'D CURB THAT IMAGINATION OF YOURS, GARFIELD

JIM DAVIS

THERE IT IS!

© 1980 United Feature Syndicate, Inc. 7-5

PREPARE TO MEET YOUR MAKER, SLUDGE MONSTER!

WHY DID YOU MANGLE THAT LIVER, GARFIELD?

IN THE INTEREST OF NATIONAL SECURITY, SIR

JIM DAVIS

© 1980 United Feature Syndicate, Inc.   7-9

MY PERSONAL FOOD TASTER

7-10

CRASH!   BONK!

GARFIELD!!!

I'M INNOCENT! I SWEAR IT!

JIM DAVIS   © 1980 United Feature Syndicate, Inc.

SLURP!

7-11
© 1980 United Feature Syndicate, Inc.

SLURP!

I THINK I STRAINED SOMETHING

JIM DAVIS

RING!

7-12

SMACK!

A LITTLE HIGH-STRUNG AREN'T WE?

I'M A CAT. SO SUE ME

JIM DAVIS
© 1980 United Feature Syndicate, Inc.

PURRRR

© 1980 United Feature Syndicate, Inc. 7-14

WOULD YOU LIKE SOMETHING TO EAT, GARFIELD?

THAT MAN CAN READ ME LIKE A BOOK

JIM DAVIS

7-15

GARFIELD!

DON'T TAKE ANOTHER STEP! THIS CHICKEN IS LOADED!

JIM DAVIS © 1980 United Feature Syndicate, Inc.

IT'S ANOTHER BRAND NEW DAY FOR GARFIELD, THE BIGGEST, BADDEST, MEANEST CAT IN THE LAND

7-16

AND HIS SIDEKICK, POOKY

THE BIGGEST, BADDEST, MEANEST TEDDY BEAR

JIM DAVIS © 1980 United Feature Syndicate, Inc.

7-17

© 1980 United Feature Syndicate, Inc. JIM DAVIS

7-18

POOKY! SPEAK TO ME! ARE YOU OKAY, FELLA?

© 1980 United Feature Syndicate, Inc.   JIM DAVIS

HEY, BOBBI BABY! WHAT'S HAPPENIN'?

7-19

YOU SAY I GOT A WRONG NUMBER? WELL FOR A WRONG NUMBER YOU SURE HAVE A SEXY VOICE. WHO IS THIS?

JIM DAVIS

OH, HI, MOM

EMBARRASSMENT CITY

© 1980 United Feature Syndicate, Inc.

SPLASH!

7-20

I'D BETTER GO UP FOR AIR

© 1980 United Feature Syndicate, Inc.

JiM DAViS

GASP!

GARFIELD, HOW WOULD YOU LIKE TO BE MY ATTACK CAT?

ME? AN ATTACK CAT?

7-21

YOU'D BE BY MY SIDE THWARTING DANGER

I'D BE BY YOUR SIDE THWARTING DANGER

ATTACKING ANYONE THREATENING

ATTACKING ANYTHING EDIBLE

JIM DAVIS © 1980 United Feature Syndicate, Inc.

I HAVE CONSTRUCTED A THUG-DUMMY FOR YOUR ATTACK TRAINING, GARFIELD

7-22

JIM DAVIS

KILL!

HA-HA-HA HA-HA!

© 1980 United Feature Syndicate, Inc.

© 1980 United Feature Syndicate, Inc.

OKAY, ATTACK CAT, LET'S SAY A MUGGER JUMPS OUT OF THE BUSHES

7-25

A 300-POUND MUGGER WITH A CLUB

HOW WILL WE EVER PROTECT OURSELVES?

HE'S NOT AFTER **MY** WALLET, JACK

© 1980 United Feature Syndicate, Inc.   JIM DAVIS

FORGET IT, GARFIELD. YOU'LL NEVER MAKE A GOOD ATTACK CAT

7-26

OH YEH? WELL JUST LET SOME BRUTE TRY TO MUG JON

I'LL GIVE HIM THE HISSING OF HIS LIFE

JIM DAVIS   © 1980 United Feature Syndicate, Inc.

7-27

JIM DAVIS

THAT'S THE THING ABOUT CANNED SALMON

HOP

IT'S EASIER TO CATCH WHEN IT HEADS UPSTREAM TO SPAWN

8-1

JIM DAVIS

GRRRR

© 1980 United Feature Syndicate, Inc.

8-2

ROWR!

ONE OF THESE DAYS THIS FIERCE ROUTINE'S GONNA GET ME CREAMED

YIP YIP YIP

JIM DAVIS

© 1980 United Feature Syndicate, Inc.

JIM DAVIS   8-3

I'M PUTTING YOU ON A DIET, GARFIELD. YOU MAY HAVE WHATEVER YOU CAN SIP THROUGH A STRAW

JIM DAVIS © 1980 United Feature Syndicate, Inc.

SUCK!

BACK TO THE DRAWING BOARD

8-4

DO YOU KNOW WHAT CONSTITUTES A DIET FOOD?

© 1980 United Feature Syndicate, Inc.

IT'S NOT THE CALORIES, IT'S NOT THE PROTEIN, IT'S NOT THE FIBER...

JIM DAVIS

IT'S THE BLAND

8-5

HOW GOES THE DIET GARFIELD?

JIM DAVIS © 1980 United Feature Syndicate, Inc.

HAVE YOU LOST ANYTHING YET?

YES

MY SENSE OF HUMOR

8-6

REMEMBER, GARFIELD, ONE DRUMSTICK A DAY ON YOUR DIET AND THAT'S IT

© 1980 United Feature Syndicate, Inc. JIM DAVIS

WHAT THE...

I FOUND A BUTCHER WHO CARRIES PTERODACTYL

8-7

DID YOU EVER OWN A CAT, LYMAN?

I GREW UP WITH FOUR OF 'EM

WHAT WERE THEIR NAMES?

8·24

LET'S SEE...

THERE WAS "CAT," "CAT," "CAT" AND "CAT"

NO NAMES?

© 1980 United Feature Syndicate, Inc.

WHAT'S THE USE OF NAMING A PET THAT WON'T COME WHEN YOU CALL IT?

GOOD POINT

JIM DAVIS

GARFIELD, THERE'S NOTHING YOU CAN DO OR SAY TO MAKE ME SHARE MY LASAGNA WITH YOU

NOW THAT WAS AN EFFECTIVE LITTLE PLOY

FLIP

FLIP!

YOU'RE A LOUSY READER, GARFIELD

YOU PLAY A LOUSY GAME OF FLIP, FELLA

JIM DAVIS

SCRATCH
SCRATCH
SCRATCH
SCRATCH
SCRATCH

© 1980 United Feature Syndicate, Inc. JIM DAVIS

WOOF
WOOF

8-30

RRRRRR

© 1980 United Feature Syndicate, Inc.

EEK, EEK, SHIVER
WITH FRIGHT, BEG FOR
MERCY, RACE UP A TREE

JIM DAVIS

JIM DAVIS

8-31

HOW IS IT YOU CATS KNOW EXACTLY WHEN TO BE UNDERFOOT?

LUCKY I GUESS

GARFIELD'S HISTORY OF DOGS

THE WORLD'S FIRST DOG CRAWLED OUT OF THE SEA ABOUT TEN MILLION YEARS AGO

9-1

BUT, UNFORTUNATELY FOR HIM ...

© 1980 United Feature Syndicate, Inc.

HE WAS IMMEDIATELY NABBED BY THE WORLD'S FIRST DOGCATCHER

JIM DAVIS

GARFIELD'S HISTORY OF DOGS

TAIL WAGGING WAS INVENTED BY A DOG NAMED "BONZO WAG"

HE FOUND TAIL WAGGING ENDEARED HIM TO HUMANS

© 1980 United Feature Syndicate, Inc.

BONZO ALSO INVENTED SLOBBERING, BUT THAT DIDN'T GO OVER SO WELL

9-2

JIM DAVIS

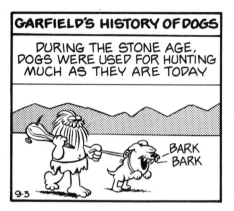

GARFIELD'S HISTORY OF DOGS

DURING THE STONE AGE, DOGS WERE USED FOR HUNTING MUCH AS THEY ARE TODAY

BARK BARK

9-3

GRRRR

© 1980 United Feature Syndicate, Inc.

TIMES WERE TOUGH THEN

STOMP!

JIM DAVIS

GARFIELD'S HISTORY OF DOGS

CONTRARY TO POPULAR BELIEF...

9-4

THE FIRST DOGS WERE **HAPPY** TO MEET THE FIRST CAT

FOR, UNTIL THEN, ALL THEY HAD TO CHASE UP TREES WERE ROCKS

ARF

© 1980 United Feature Syndicate, Inc.

JIM DAVIS

GARFIELD'S HISTORY OF DOGS

JIM DAVIS © 1980 United Feature Syndicate, Inc.

THE FIRST FIRE HYDRANT

9-5

DOGS' HISTORIC ROLES AS HUNTERS, PROTECTORS, TRACKERS, LABORERS AND COMPANIONS HAVE CULMINATED TO MAKE MODERN DOG WHAT HE IS TODAY

JIM DAVIS © 1980 United Feature Syndicate, Inc.

IT COULD JUST MAKE YOU CRY

9-6

DO YOU FEEL PERSONALLY RESPONSIBLE FOR THE WORLD FOOD SHORTAGE?

EVERY TIME YOU GO TO THE BEACH, DOES THE TIDE COME IN?

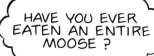

HAVE YOU EVER EATEN AN ENTIRE MOOSE?

CAN YOU SEE YOUR NECK?

© 1980 United Feature Syndicate, Inc.

DO JOGGERS TAKE LAPS AROUND YOU FOR EXERCISE?

IF SO, WELCOME TO **NATIONAL FAT WEEK!**

JIM DAViS

9-7

THIS WEEK WE'LL EAT WITHOUT GUILT, AND KICK OFF OUR MEMBERSHIP CAMPAIGN...

BY FORCE-FEEDING A BOX OF CORNSTARCH TO A SKINNY PERSON

WELCOME TO NATIONAL FAT WEEK.

9-8

THIS IS THE WEEK ALL OF YOU, MY FAT BROTHERS AND SISTERS, CELEBRATE YOUR BIG, ROUND, BEAUTIFUL BODIES

REMEMBER, YOU'RE NOT OVERWEIGHT, EVERYONE ELSE IS UNDERNOURISHED

© 1980 United Feature Syndicate, Inc.   JIM DAVIS

THIS IS NATIONAL FAT WEEK. ARISE, FAT PEOPLE!

9-9

LET US AVERT OUR NATION'S INSENSITIVITY TOWARD FAT PEOPLE!

LET US MAKE FUN OF BALD PEOPLE!

© 1980 United Feature Syndicate, Inc.   JIM DAVIS

HERE'S A NATIONAL FAT WEEK HANDY FACT...

9-10

60% OF THE PEOPLE IN OUR NATION ARE INVOLVED IN SOME WAY WITH THE FOOD INDUSTRY

THAT'S RIGHT. EATING IS NOT ONLY FUN, IT'S PATRIOTIC!

© 1980 United Feature Syndicate, Inc.   JIM DAVIS

THIS YEAR, LET'S CELEBRATE NATIONAL FAT WEEK BY STAMPING OUT FAT JOKES

9-11

LET'S FACE IT, FATTIES...

WE SHOULD BE ABLE TO STAMP OUT ANYTHING WE WISH

© 1980 United Feature Syndicate, Inc.   JIM DAVIS

WE FAT PEOPLE ARE CONSTANTLY BEING DISCRIMINATED AGAINST

9-12

AIRPLANE AND THEATER SEATS ARE TOO SMALL. DESIGNER CLOTHING IS NOT MADE IN OUR SIZE. BUT THAT'S TRIVIAL.

WHAT THIS WORLD REALLY NEEDS IS A KING-SIZE SANDBOX

JIM DAVIS © 1980 United Feature Syndicate, Inc.

HERE'S A NATIONAL FAT WEEK DIET JOKE:

9-13

WHAT WOULD YOU GET IF YOU CROSS A DIETER WITH A NINE-FOOT GORILLA?

YOU GET A GORILLA WHO DIETS ANYWHERE HE PLEASES

© 1980 United Feature Syndicate, Inc. JIM DAVIS

OH, GARFIEEELD ♪

GO FETCH THE PAPER

YOU GOTTA BE KIDDING

NO PAPER, NO BREAKFAST

THAT'S BLACKMAIL

GOOD BOY!

© 1980 United Feature Syndicate, Inc.

9-14

JiM DAViS

WOULD YOU LIKE TO GO OUT, GARFIELD?

© 1980 United Feature Syndicate, Inc.

9-19

POW!

OR WOULD YOU RATHER STAY IN?

JIM DAVIS

9-20

YOU LOOK GUILTY ABOUT SOMETHING, GARFIELD

DID YOU EAT MY PIE?

YOUR PEPPER STEAK

© 1980 United Feature Syndicate, Inc.

JIM DAVIS

9-24 JIM DAVIS

SPLOT!

© 1980 United Feature Syndicate, Inc.

LET ME GUESS. YOU'RE TRYING TO TELL ME YOU DON'T LIKE YOUR MEAL

IN MY OWN SUBTLE WAY

WE CATS ARE VERY UNIQUE

JIM DAVIS 9-25

WHO ELSE HAS OUR PRIDE, STYLE AND SOPHISTICATION?

© 1980 United Feature Syndicate, Inc.

WHO ELSE CAN KILL AN AFTERNOON HANGING ON THE SCREEN DOOR?

9-26

© 1980 United Feature Syndicate, Inc.   JIM DAVIS

9-27   JIM DAVIS

© 1980 United Feature Syndicate, Inc.

HMMM, JON'S GOLF CAP

NO ONE DRIVES FASTER THAN THE GREAT ENZIO BODONI!

ALMS FOR A TAP DANCING CAT

TAPPITY TAPPITY

CHECK THAT OIL, MISTER?

QUACK QUACK QUACK

© 1980 United Feature Syndicate, Inc.

10-5

SOMETIMES I WORRY ABOUT YOU, GARFIELD

HA HA HA HA

JIM DAVIS

CATS ARE GREAT TO SLEEP WITH ON CHILLY NIGHTS

JIM DAVIS

SCRATCH
SCRATCH
SCRATCH
SCRATCH

© 1980 United Feature Syndicate, Inc.

IF YOU CAN PUT UP WITH SOME OF THEIR ECCENTRICITIES

10-10

CATS ARE NOT ONLY CUTE AND FUZZY...

JIM DAVIS

WE ALSO MAKE KEEN ALARM CLOCKS

© 1980 United Feature Syndicate, Inc.

AT NO EXTRA CHARGE

10-11

KICK!

© 1980 United Feature Syndicate, Inc.

WHERE DID NERMAL GO?

HE'S TAKING A SHORT NAP

JIM DAVIS

CLOP   CLOP

JIM DAVIS

HA HA, CATS ARE SO CUTE WHEN THEY PLAY DRESS-UP

© 1980 United Feature Syndicate, Inc.

CUTE TO A POINT, THAT IS

10-18

SCRATCH
SCRATCH
SCRATCH

GARFIELD, WHAT WOULD YOU SAY IF I SAID MY CHAIR IS DAMAGED?

I'D SAY YOU'RE RIGHT

WHAT WOULD YOU SAY IF I SAID THE DAMAGE LOOKS LIKE IT WAS DONE BY A CAT?

I'D SAY THERE DO APPEAR TO BE SOME ABRASIONS OF THE CLAW PERSUASION

© 1980 United Feature Syndicate, Inc.

WHAT WOULD YOU SAY IF I SAID WE BOTH KNOW THIS CAT?

I'D SAY YOU'RE GETTING WARM

WHAT WOULD YOU SAY IF I SAID **YOU** ARE THE CAT WHO SCRATCHED MY CHAIR?

I'D SAY THAT IS A DISTINCT POSSIBILITY

10-19

WHAT WOULD YOU SAY IF I SAID NEVER SHARPEN YOUR CLAWS ON MY CHAIR AGAIN?

NO COMPRENDO, SEÑOR

JIM DAVIS

SCRATCH
SCRATCH
SCRATCH
SCRATCH

10-20

SCRATCH
SCRATCH
SCRATCH
SCRATCH

JIM DAVIS

ME, GARFIELD THE CAT,
A WALKING FLEA CIRCUS.
WHAT A BUMMER

I DON'T MIND
THE ITCHING
OR BITING

BUT THE LIGHTS
FROM THE MIDWAY
ARE KEEPING
ME AWAKE

10-21

JIM DAVIS

10-29

TIP

JIM DAVIS © 1980 United Feature Syndicate, Inc.

10-30

WAKA WAKA WAKA WAKA WAKA WAKA

© 1980 United Feature Syndicate, Inc.

JIM DAVIS

10-31

JiM DAViS © 1980 United Feature Syndicate, Inc.

11-1

© 1980 United Feature Syndicate, Inc. JiM DAViS

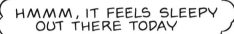

HMMM, IT FEELS SLEEPY OUT THERE TODAY

YOU'RE LOOKING A LITTLE LISTLESS, GARFIELD

I PREFER TO THINK OF IT AS AN ADVANCED STATE OF RELAXATION

I'M TAKING YOU TO THE VET

THEY HAVE A CURE FOR LAZY?

HIS GET UP AND GO GOT UP AND WENT, DOC

IT'S NOTHING A LITTLE CATNAP COULDN'T FIX

A VITAMIN SHOT SHOULD DO THE TRICK

© 1980 United Feature Syndicate, Inc.   11-2

BUT YOU DIDN'T EVEN GIVE HIM THE SHOT

IT'S THE THOUGHT THAT COUNTS

TAPPITY   TAPPITY   TAPPITY   TAPPITY   TAPPITY

JIM DAVIS

About Jim Davis, creator of GARFIELD

Jim Davis was born July 28, 1945, in Marion, Indiana. After growing up on a farm near Fairmount, Indiana, with about 25 cats, Jim attended Ball State University in Muncie. As an Art and Business major he distinguished himself by earning one of the lowest accumulative grade point averages in the history of the university.

During a two-year stint at a local advertising agency Jim met and married wife, Carolyn, a gifted singer and elementary school teacher.

In 1969 he became the assistant to Tom Ryan on the syndicated comic strip, TUMBLEWEEDS. In addition to cartooning, Jim maintained a career as a freelance commercial artist, copywriter, and radio-talent and political-campaign promoter.

His hobbies include chess, sandwiches, and good friends. A new pastime is playing with his two-year-old son, James Alexander.

In 1978 United Feature Syndicate gave the nod to GARFIELD.

Jim explains, "GARFIELD is strictly an entertainment strip built around the strong personality of a fat, lazy, cynical cat. It's the funniest strip I've ever seen. GARFIELD consciously avoids any social or political comment. My grasp of the world situation isn't that firm anyway. For years, I thought OPEC was a denture adhesive."

The strip is pumped out daily, in a cheerful atmosphere among friends. Valette Hildebrand is assistant cartoonist, Brian Strater is art director for merchandising, Neil Altekruse is production director, Jill Hahn is office manager, and Julie Hamilton is president of Paws, Incorporated, the company that handles the merchandising of the characters in the strip.

"To what do I attribute my cartooning ability?" Jim asks. "As a child I was asthmatic. I was stuck indoors with little more than my imagination and paper and pencil to play with. While asthma worked for me, I wouldn't recommend it for everyone.

"Do I like cartooning?...It's nice work if you can get it."